First U.S. Edition 1981 by Barron's Educational Series, Inc.

Published in France under the title *Mon Livre de Mots de tous les jours*
© Flammarion, 1977
English translation © J.M. Dent & Sons Ltd 1978

All inquiries should be addressed to:
Barron's Educational Series, Inc.
250 Wireless Boulevard
Hauppauge, New York 11788

Library of Congress Catalog Card No. 79-89631

International Standard Book No. 0-8120-5344-3

PRINTED IN HONG KONG

123   490   13 12 11

BENVENUTI

My Everyday
FRENCH
Word Book

Text by Michèle Kahn

Translated by Gwen Marsh

BARRON'S

New York • London • Toronto • Sydney

Le Réveil   Waking Up

Seven o'clock! Yes, it's seven o'clock all right, but what day is it? I'm all mixed up about the days ... Yesterday Mommy and Daddy took us to see Grandpa and Grandma in the country. That was Sunday. So today must be Monday, and I shall have to get up and dress for school.

I can hear Daddy making the coffee in the kitchen. Mommy is washing in the bathroom.

le lit

la fenêtre

le pyjama

le rideau

une casquette

une chemise

la lampe

l'oreiller

le réveil

la couverture

le livre

la table de nuit

le drap

une chaussette

un slip

un tabouret

le tapis

le pantalon

un soulier

6

l'armoire

un dessin

le radiateur

la ficelle

une lampe

le papier

une gomme

un crayon

la chaise

un Indien

un soldat

un cavalier

7

Debout! Up We Get!

Ça y est : je suis levé !
Now I'm up.

Je mets mes pantoufles.
I put on my slippers.

J'ouvre la porte.
I open the door.

Je marche dans le couloir.
I walk down the hall.

Ma sœur dort encore.
My sister is still asleep.

Je tire le rideau.
I draw the curtain.

Laure ouvre les yeux.
Laura opens her eyes.

Elle bâille.
She yawns.

Elle me sourit.
She smiles at me.

La Chambre de Laure   Laura's Room

I am older than Laura. Every morning when my alarm goes off I have to wake my little sister. I shake her teddy bear and dolls, shouting, "Time to get up!"

Laura always sits the big doll in the middle, between the baby and the middle-sized doll. She says the big doll is the mother of the other two. Yesterday Grandma gave Laura some sewing things. I'd like to learn to sew, as well. I could make myself some shoes like Indians wear: moccasins. "Laura, will you lend me your needle and thread?"

"Yes, if you will help me build a nice house for my dolls!"

"All right, I'll try and find a big cardboard box," says Robert.

un abat-jour

une robe

une chemise de nuit

la prise de courant

une pantoufle

les ciseaux

une poupée

un sac

la laine

une ceinture

un dé

le tiroir

un pouf

un ours en peluche

la commode

le fauteuil

une sandale

9

La Toilette   Washing

Je me brosse les dents.
I brush my teeth.

Puis je me lave.
Then I wash myself.

Après, je me coiffe.
After that, I comb my hair.

Now it's my turn in the bathroom. In the mornings I have to be quick, so I usually have my bath at night.

First, I brush my teeth. I like the taste of the toothpaste. Then I wash. The soap smells good. Last of all, I brush and comb my hair, so that it looks neat.

After that, I stand in front of the mirror to dress myself. If you don't look at what you are doing, you might put your clothes on back to front, or do up the buttons in the wrong button holes!

10

Je m'habille   I Get Dressed

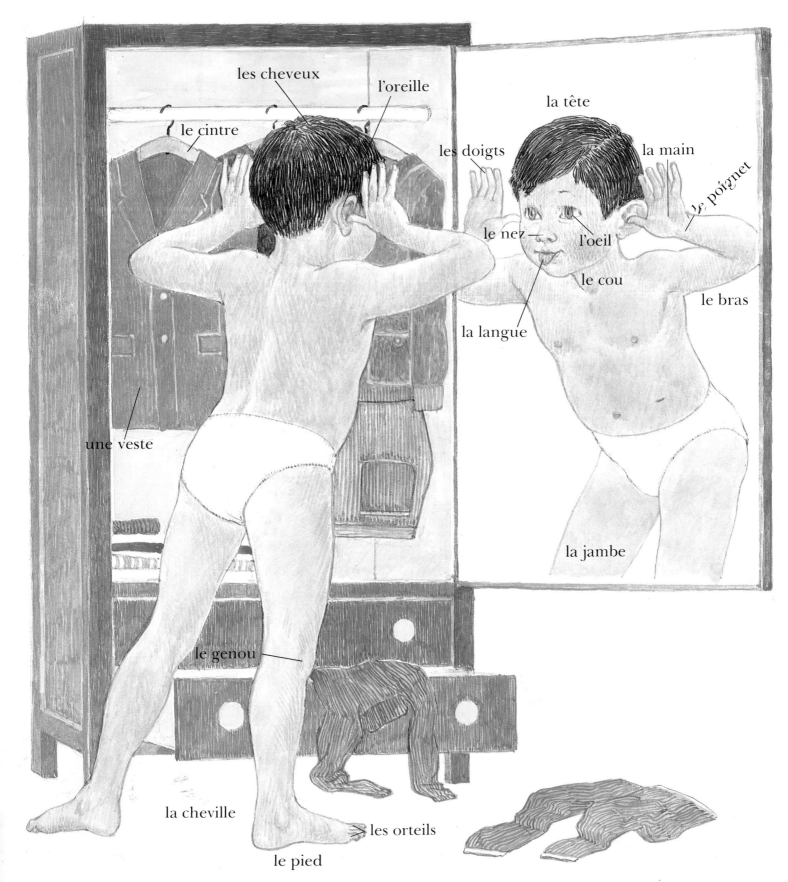

les cheveux

l'oreille

le cintre

la tête

les doigts

la main

le poignet

le nez

l'oeil

le cou

le bras

la langue

une veste

la jambe

le genou

la cheville

les orteils

le pied

Et enfin, je m'habille devant la glace.
I get dressed in front of the mirror.

Le Petit Déjeuner   Breakfast

Eight o'clock. There isn't much time for breakfast. We have to leave for school soon. I can smell the coffee and toast. Usually we all have milk. Sometimes one of us has tea or chocolate. Breakfast is my favorite meal.

la bouilloire

le grille-pain

la cuisinière

les allumettes

le four

le réfrigérateur

le couteau

la cafetière

la cuiller

la fourchette

le sucre

le lait

le pain

un chat

le panier

l'assiette

le beurre

le jus d'orange

la tasse

un presse-citron

la confiture

la soucoupe

12

la table

La Maison The House

la cheminée

le grenier

une chambre

le balcon

la salle
de bains

une chambre

une chambre

la cuisine

la pièce de séjour

l'entrée

le garage

13

le toit

le volet

la lanterne

la porte

le lierre

la marche

l'allée

14

Le Jardin   The Garden

Every morning Mommy and Daddy kiss us goodbye. They tell us to be very careful crossing the road. I take Laura's hand and we run as fast as we can to the garden gate. Laura laughs. "I'm flying!" she shouts. Patch barks as we pass. It's his way of joining in the fun.

un arbre

le lilas

une haie

une feuille

un kiosque

la tondeuse

la boîte aux lettres

le portail

une rose

l'herbe

la chaîne

le chien

un oiseau

la niche

15

un autobus

la boulangerie

une moto

le feu

un camion

une auto

la roue

le trottoir

le passage
protégé

la bicyclette

les piétons

un agent de police

La Rue The Street

How difficult it is crossing a road! Luckily there is a policeman with a whistle. Otherwise the drivers would never stop to let us cross. But we are in a hurry, too. We have to be at school at nine o'clock.

16

L' École   School

la carte du monde

une horloge

l'Amérique du Nord

l'Europe

l'Asie

l'Afrique

l'Amérique du Sud

l'Océanie

le tableau

une règle

un cartable

un stylo

une trousse

un cahier

un bureau

17

La Récréation Playtime

Dix heures ! Vive la récréation ! Qui court le plus vite ?
Ten o'clock! Hurray, it's playtime! Who can run fastest?

Laure a perdu son bracelet.
Laura has lost her bracelet.

All the children look for it.

Yves tombe et se fait mal.
Yves falls and hurts himself.

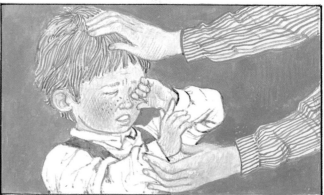

Il pleure. La maîtresse le console.
He cries. The teacher comforts him.

Vincent a trouvé le bracelet !
Vincent has found the bracelet!

Laure est de nouveau gaie.
Laura is happy again.

Nous faisons une ronde.
Round we go holding hands.

La cloche sonne. Nous nous mettons en rangs.
The bell rings. We form into lines.

Peinture . . . et Musique   Painting . . . and Music

At eleven o'clock we have our art and music lesson. Some of us learn music, while others paint and draw. There are even some who do both at once. But you can't paint with a flute or blow through a paint brush!

In the drawing lesson we draw and paint whatever we like: a tiger, a submarine, a tree or a windmill. But in the music lesson we don't just play anything. That would make a horrible noise. In music you have to play the notes that are written down.

le pinceau

le chiffon

la palette

les couleurs

le crayon-feutre

le papier à dessin

l'aquarelle

20

la trompette

la viole

le piano

les cymbales

le violon

la guitare

la flûte

le pupitre

l'électrophone

21

Le Supermarché The Supermarket

Noon. Time to go shopping. Laura and I are allowed to go to the supermarket on our own. We buy bread and milk — sometimes butter, eggs and salt. It is difficult to count out the right amount of money. The cashier should not make mistakes, but we must add it up too, just to be sure.

des fraises

des citrons

le chou-fleur

des asperges

des pommes de terre

des bananes

des prunes

des carottes

des oignons

des concombres

des poires

une pastèque

des tomates

des navets

des courgettes

des pommes

des oranges

des salades

de l'ail

du céleri

des œufs

des fromages

le lait

le beurre

la caissière

la caisse

le pain

le caddie

le porte-monnaie

22

la balance

le boucher

une horloge

de la viande

du poisson

un balai

un filet à provisions

23

Quel sera le Métier de Laure?

What Will Laura Be When She Grows Up?

… médecin ?

… danseuse ?

… photographe ?

… fleuriste ?

… secrétaire ?

24 … maîtresse ?

… ou libraire ?

Et mon Métier à moi?　And What Shall I Be?

… garagiste ?

… cosmonaute ?

… chef d'orchestre ?

… agriculteur ?

… coureur automobile ?

… pharmacien ?

… ou cuisinier ?

les couverts

Le Déjeuner Lunch

We usually have lunch at one o'clock. Everyone helps, except Daddy, who is telephoning a friend. I set the table. Laura brings in the cold dishes. She might burn herself with the hot ones. Today we must eat quickly. This afternoon we are going on a trip.

"Too bad if anyone's late," the teacher said. "The bus will leave at two o'clock sharp."

la vapeur

le poulet

le plat

l'assiette

la marmite

la bouteille

la serviette

le verre

la carafe

le saladier

la nappe

le journal

le fauteuil

le tablier

le téléphone

En Route!
We're Off!

le panneau de signalisation

le rétroviseur

le chauffeur

l'essuie-glace

le pare-brise

la vitre

le volant

la pendule

le tableau de bord

la banquette

27

La Campagne The Country

What a long way you can see when you're in the country! Here we are on a hill. Down below, in the valley, there is a village.
'Look at the squirrel in the tree!' shouts Vincent.

l'église

la rivière

la gare

le train

le pont

la voie ferrée

le ruisseau

la route

le parapet

It's lovely to be in the country. You can hear the birds singing. You can fish in the river. You can paddle, too. I would like to stay in the country forever.

le champ

l'écureuil

la canne à pêche

les bottes

le rocher

29

La Ferme   The Farm

It's three o'clock already. Soon we shall have to go home. But I would much rather stay at this farm a little longer – driving the tractor, looking at the cows in the fields, pushing the wheelbarrow and climbing the haystack. And I want to help the farmer's wife feed the chickens. I like all kinds of animals, not only the ones here on the farm, but also the wild animals we saw at the zoo last week.

la charrue

le foin

la fourche

un veau

une vach

la brouette

un cochon

la queue

un cheval

un canard

une oie

un caneton

30

un fermier

le tracteur

une pompe

un dindon

un seau

le chariot

un coq

des grains

une fermière

une poule

des poussins

31

un éléphant

l'eau

un paon

un cygne

un perroquet

une cage

un singe

Au Zoo   At the Zoo

In this picture you can see an elephant blowing water out of his trunk, a peacock spreading his tail, a crocodile sleeping beside the pool, a parrot squawking in its cage, a swan gliding on the water, a lion roaring and a giraffe browsing on the leaves of a tall tree. A monkey eats a banana while another swings by his tail.

l'enclos

un crocodile

une lionne et
ses lionceaux

un lion

une girafe

33

un drapeau

une pelle

un château de sable

un coquillage

un tunnel

le car

La Mer   The Sea

As soon as the weather is fine, tourists come and stay in our part of the country. We are lucky enough to live near the sea. When I go to the beach, I build sandcastles. I usually build them with battlements and put a little flag on top. I swim with a life preserver. When the sea is not rough, Daddy and Mommy take us sailing.

un voilier

un bateau à vapeur

un phare

un hors-bord

la plage

un bateau de pêche

une valise

des rames

la montagne

un tunnel

une locomotive
électrique

un fourgon

un wagon de
marchandises

la barriè

36

un avion

un nuage

la fumée

une voiture de voyageurs

un parapluie

le passage à niveau

Le Train   The Train

Here is the four o'clock train. We arrive at the grade crossing just in time to see it go by. "Look at the signalman's house!" Laura says to me. "I'd like to make one like that for my dolls." What a good idea! Oh look, it's raining now.

une cabane

une table de ping-pong

une raquette de ping-pong

une raquette de tennis

la glace

la balle

le ballon

la corde à sauter

une trottinette

le patin à roulettes

Les Jeux   Games

Five o'clock. Home at last, Mommy gives us each an ice cream. Laura and I play games in the garden. Laura puts on her roller skates and I ride on the scooter. Then we play soccer until it's time to watch television.

38

La Télévision Television

La télévision est éteinte.
The television is off.

Je l'allume.
I turn it on.

La speakerine annonce…
… un film qui se passe en hiver.
The announcer introduces a film
about a winter holiday.

la montagne

la neige

des flocons de neige

une boule de neige

un bonhomme de neige

un skieur

une enfant-luge

des sapins

un chalet

un gâteau

un tire-bouchon

une mont[re]

un plateau
de fromages

un balai

un aspirateur

Le Dîner Dinner

Seven o'clock. We are having dinner on our own this evening
because Daddy and Mommy are giving a party. Mommy has
put on an apron to protect her pretty dress.

Le Soir   Evening

At eight o'clock Laura comes into my room and we read a book together. It is already dark outside. Soon, Mommy and Daddy will take Laura to her own bed. "Good night! Sweet dreams," they say. Laura calls out, "One more kiss!" and I shout, "Me, too." Mommy and Daddy pretend to be cross. But they kiss us all the same. Then we go to sleep to make tomorrow come quickly.

Index

Note: The gender of the noun is shown by (m) *masculine*, or (f) *feminine*.

presse-citron *m* lemon squeezer, juicer 12
prise de courant *f* electric plug 9
prune *f* plum 22
pupitre *m* desk or music stand 21
pyjama *m* pajamas 6

Q

queue *f* tail 30

R

radiateur *m* radiator 7
rame *f* oar 35
raquette de ping-pong *f* ping pong paddle 38
raquette de tennis *f* tennis racket 38
récréation *f* playtime 18
réfrigérateur *m* refrigerator 12
règle *f* ruler 17
rétroviseur *m* rearview mirror 27
réveil *m* awakening, alarm clock 6
rideau *m* curtain 6
rivière *f* river 28
robe *f* dress 9
robinet *m* faucet 10
rocher *m* rock 29
rose *f* rose 15
roue *f* wheel 16
route *f* road 27, 28
rue *f* street 16
ruisseau *m* stream 29

S

sac *m* handbag 9
salade *f* lettuce 22
saladier *m* salad bowl 26
salle de bains *f* bathroom 13
sandale *f* sandal 9
sapin *m* fir tree 39
savon *m* soap 10
seau *m* bucket 31
secrétaire *m & f* secretary 24
serviette *f* towel, napkin 10, 26
singe *m* monkey 32
skieur *m* skier 39
slip *m* underpants 6
soldat *m* soldier 7
soir *m* evening 41
soucoupe *f* saucer 12
soulier *m* shoe 6
stylo *m* pen (fountain or ball-point) 17
sucre *m* sugar 12
supermarché *m* supermarket 22

T

table *f* table 12
table de nuit *f* night table 6
table de ping-pong *f* ping pong table 38
tableau *m* board 17
tableau de bord *m* dashboard 27
tablier *m* apron 26
tabouret *m* stool 6
tapis *m* mat, carpet 6
tasse *f* cup 12
téléphone *m* telephone 26
télévision *f* television 39
tête *f* head 11
tire-bouchon *m* corkscrew 40
tiroir *m* drawer 9
toilette *f* washing and dressing 10
toit *m* roof 14
tomate *f* tomato 22
tondeuse *f* mower 15
tracteur *m* tractor 31
train *m* train 28, 37
trompette *f* trumpet 21
trottinette *f* scooter 38
trottoir *m* sidewalk 16
trousse *f* pen and pencil case 17
tunnel *m* tunnel 34, 36

V

vache *f* cow 30
valise *f* suitcase 35
vapeur *f* steam 26
veau *m* calf 30
verre *m* glass 26
veste *f* jacket 11
viande *f* meat 23
viole *f* viola 21
violon *m* violin 21
vitre *f* windowpane 27
voie ferrée *f* railway track 28
voilier *m* sailboat 35
voiture de voyageurs *f* passenger car 37
volant *m* steering wheel 27
volet *m* shutter 14

W

wagon de marchandises *m* box car 36

Z

zoo *m* zoo 32